ONE PENNY OPERA

ONE-PENNY OPERA

A Musical Parody
In
One Act

By
Lindy Wall

Cover Art by L.E. Wall

Cover Design by Wienerdog Studios

Libretto published in 2007 by

FUTUROLA, INCORPORATED
P. O. Box 15181
Savannah, GA 31416

All rights reserved. Copyright 2007 Lindy Wall

This libretto is protected by copyright. Any unauthorized publication, reproduction, broadcast, public performance, copying, taping or recording in any manner whatsoever, including such actions without monetary gain, without the express permission of the librettist or publisher will constitute infringement of copyright and will render the infringer liable to an action of law.
No part of this work may be transmitted in any form or by any means, graphic, electronic, or mechanical, or by any information storage or retrieval system, without the permission in writing from the librettist or publisher, except in the case of brief questions embodied in critical articles or reviews.

Published 2007
Printed in the United States of America

ISBN 978-0-6151-8893-5

Cover Art Copyright 2007 Wienerdog Studios

ONE PENNY OPERA

CONTENTS

CAST OF CHARACTERS

SONG LIST

SYNOPSIS

LIBRETTO

LYRICS

CAST OF CHARACTERS

RENALDO, MALE RABBIT
RAISA, FEMALE RABBIT
PERCIVAL, MALE OPOSSUM
ELGAR, MALE EAGLE
CIRILLO, MALE CAT
ROSSINI, MALE RAT
RACHEL, FEMALE RAT
SOLANGE, FEMALE SQUIRREL
SIEGFRIED, MALE SQUIRREL
DEMETRIUS, MALE DOG
FRANCESCA, FEMALE FROG
CLARESSA, FEMALE CAT
CECIL, MALE CRAWFISH
ESME, FEMALE EAGLE
DEMOSTHENES, MALE DOVE
DONATELLA, FEMALE DOVE
SEAGULLS and CROWS (voices only, for puppets)
THOR, MALE TURTLE
FERDINAND, MALE FROG
DANTE, MALE DEER
TESSA, FEMALE TURTLE
CASSANDRA, FEMALE CRAWFISH
FAISAL, MALE FISH
DIANA, FEMALE DOG
FIONA, FEMALE FISH
HENLEY, MALE HUMAN
HETTA, FEMALE HUMAN
DESDEMONA, FEMALE DEER
MALE FLEA (voice only)
FEMALE FLEA (voice only)
PENELOPE, FEMALE OPOSSUM

SONG LIST

NO-SEE'UMS
IF I ONLY HAD A MATE
PRIDE OF THE PREDATORS
GENES, GLORIOUS GENES
GENEALOGY OVERTURE
I ENJOY BEING A SQUIRREL
I'M GETTING FEATHERS
FRESH POULTRY
JUST ENOUGH
MY FLAVORED THINGS
MAD ABOUT BERRIES
GIRL MARSUPIAL
HAVE YOURSELF A BERRY-FLAVORED YOGHURT
BRIE NEARLY WAS MINE
THE HOLES ARE ALIVE
HUNKY-DORY
MARCH OF THE HAWKS AND EAGLES
EASY TO FIND SEEDS
GOLDEN EAGLE/SIMPLY A NEST
NEST IN DORMERS
BIRD POO BECOMES YOU
BLOWFLIES OVER THE ROAD-KILL ON ROVER
FLIES BE GONE
IT'S A SWELL TIDE FOR SWIMMING
SILVER MINNOWS
SOMEWHERE IN MY TAD- OR EGGHOOD
WHAT A WICKED COOK IS MAN
OKRA GUMBO!
I 'SPECT THAT'S WHY THEY CALL IT A STEW

SONG LIST (continued)

LUNCHEON FARE
A BEATING HEART
I FEEL ICKY
CATPAN
NEITHER A TOM CAT NOR A MOM CAT BE
A PARASITE'S LIFE FER FLEAS
FLEAS MUST GO
HOW DO YOU LOSE A NUISANCE LIKE A FLEA-AH?
I'LL BE FLEAING YOU
WALK LIKE AN OPOSSUM
EE-YOW!

SYNOPSIS

ONE PENNY OPERA

Around the beached and partially buried wreckage of an ark, a small coastal community of creatures has formed, living ordinary lives and facing the common challenge of finding food without becoming it. Despite the inevitable tension between prey and predatory animals, and the occasional challenge of parasite infestation, their lives are pleasant, made more so by the fact that they exist in pairs ... except for the opossum, whose mate has inexplicably vanished.

Day passes into evening, night progresses to dawn, and evening arrives again. The diurnal and nocturnal denizens meet at the fresh water hole formed by an inlet from the sea. They interact occasionally even when it is time for some to be sleeping, and all accept that they must coexist.

The broken ship, its hatch covers and scattered, rotting, cargo crates provide shelter for the animals. To the west, the bow of the ark juts out, with waves and small rafts of sargassum and other sea grasses lapping at its hull. The stern of the ark is almost completely buried by sand and scrub vegetation, with only the transom and a small amount of decking visible. Behind the stern there is an expanse of barren ground, and above it in the distance is a sprawling eagle's nest.

A trickle of ocean meanders through marsh and grasses towards the east, to form a brackish marsh and then a small potable water hole in the center of the area. As the land firms eastward, there is more substantial vegetation, in progression from marsh grass to scrub palmettos to fruit and nut trees, a few scrubby magnolias, ferns, and lusher grasses. Rudimentary signs of human occupation exist in the eastern area. They include a large garbage dumpster at a distance behind the water hole, a street sign reading "Rover Street", and one corner of a dilapidated screened porch, raised above the marsh grass on pilings, with one screen panel shredded. Animals can go in and out of the porch through the damaged panel, and a cat litter box within is visible.

ACT ONE
(The One and Only Act)

The sun is low in the western sky. A male rabbit and his mate lament their encounter with a swarm of gnats. They join other animals at the watering hole. A male opossum sets out on his nightly food gathering as he ponders his solitary life. Just as the sun appears in the east, after a successful night of foraging, he settles in his nest. A male eagle and male cat announce their arrivals with braggado regarding their ancestry and predatory prowess, evoking a lively discussion of genealogy among all the animals. The squirrels count the reasons they enjoy life, doves bemoan their molting, and carnivores contemplate how tasty the doves might be.

As all the animals compare the things that bring them happiness – foods in the most part – the opossum shares the story of how he met, and lost, his mate. To cheer him, some of the scavengers produce an assortment of tasty bits gleaned from the humans' party on the next street. They dream of the large platters of gourmet foods they nearly made off with as the partiers imbibed. The male eagle swoops in, and the prey animals dive into safe places. They venture out, again, philosophical about their fears and the devices they use to avoid the predators, but saddened by the eagles' ferocious nature.

The female eagle in their aerie tends eaglets as she mocks her mate's pomposity. The doves speak of their own choices of nesting areas. The female dog enjoys a good roll in guano, causing consternation among some of the other creatures. When a bath is suggested, the fish in the intended bathwater – the surf – protest. They want to swim without suds, and their antics inspire the turtles to voice their love of minnows.

Two frogs leap out of reach of the snapping turtle beaks, only to confront a pair of salivating humans wielding chef's knives and frying pans. The omnivorous inclinations of the humans provoke considerable lamentation among the animals. Forever pursued by humans and other carnivores, the prey animals feel like little more than snack fare. The cats and dogs have their own problems, being perpetually on the hunt for game. Feline furball maladies and haughty manners give way to the annoyances of parasite infestation.

Once again the benefits of a mate are made clear to all of the animals, as each grooms the other to remove pests. The solitary male opossum sadly grooms himself. The sun drops and the moon rises, bathing the opossum in a blue-white light as the paired animals fall into silhouette. From beneath the porch a small, misshapen figure emerges, and heads for the male opossum. As the moonlight illuminates more of the ground, the male opossum is stunned to see than the odd little figure is his mate. He greets her and finds four baby opossums clinging to her back. All of the animals rejoice with the reunited couple.

LIBRETTO

NO-SEE'UMS

The sun is low in the sky. Orange and pink light washes over the west as the east darkens. The sunset illuminates a lone, agitated figure perched upon the bow of the ark wreckage. He is joined by his mate.

RENALDO RABBIT
No-see'ums ...
I just hit a cloud of no-see'ums,
And suddenly it's plain
They've carried my poor brain away.

RAISA RABBIT
No-see'ums ...
There's just no escaping no-see'ums.
They get into my ears,
And places that I dare not say.

RENALDO AND RAISA
No-see'ums ...

RENALDO
Run away when you see them swarming.

RAISA
Get the spray, or you'll itch until morning.

RENALDO
No-see'ums ...
I find them alarming,
No-see'ums.

IF I ONLY HAD A MATE

The rabbits join other animals milling around the water hole at dusk. The sun disappears in the west and a full moon peeks over the eastern horizon. Diurnal creatures leave for their beds, as the nocturnals begin to roam.
A male opossum skirts the group. As he forages, placing his food finds in a rusty children's sand bucket, the moon travels quickly across the sky. It is still visible low in the western sky as dawn breaks and the opossum returns to breakfast in his nest.

PERCIVAL 'POSSUM, *strolling around with a battered child's sand bucket*
Oh, the water hole is hoppin'.
Everyone is stoppin'
By for a drink.
Got to watch for dogs and owl-ers,
And the other evenin' prowlers,
But I'm faster than they think.

Gee, the night is dark and eerie,
And I'm kind of leery
Of wanderin' far from home.
Wouldn't mind bein' nocturnal
If it weren't for this infernal
State of bein' alone.

He finds treats at the outer base of the dumpster.

Dum-de-dum-de-da-de-dada –
Ooh, a ripe banana!
Mm–
Mm–
Mmm!
La-de-da-de-dum-de-doodle,
Here's a pack of ramen noodles!
I shall have them for brunch.

He puts a banana in the bucket, and another, and a third banana.
He puts wadded butcher paper parcel in the bucket, followed by ramen noodles.

Now the mornin' sun is risin'.
Time to close my eyes, an'
I don't wanna be late.
Oh, my nest is comfy-cozy,
And the whole world would be rosy ...
If I only had a mate.

PRIDE OF THE PREDATORS

As nocturnal and diurnal animals mingle again at the water hole, a male eagle and male cat arrive, compelling the prey animals to seek shelter. The predators brag of their inherent prowess, and several rodents grow tired of the litany. Their mocking comments cause the eagle and cat to swivel their heads back and forth as they shoot threatening glares at the taunting prey.

ELGAR EAGLE, *spreading his wings*
I am a raptor.
I am descended
From pterodactyls.
I am the best.

CIRILLO CAT, *stretching his long body*
I am descended
From mighty tigers.
I am ferocious.

RENALDO RABBIT, *from his hole*
Oh, give it a rest!

ROSSINI AND RACHEL RAT, *imitative, as they scurry up to the bow of the ark*
Nyah, nyah-nyah-nyah, nyah,
Nyah, nyah-nyah-nyah, nyah …

GENES, GLORIOUS GENES

Inspired by the predators' claims to great ancestry, rodents and others celebrate evolution. As the others sing and dance around, the female rabbit line-dances behind the others, with three (puppet) rabbit children on each side, mimicking their mother's movements. Halfway through the song, the female disappears, sheds her kids, and reappears to mingle with the other animals.

RENALDO RABBIT, ROSSINI and RACHEL RAT, SOLANGE and SIEGFRIED SQUIRREL
Genes, glorious genes!
Your DNA's showin'.

DEMETRIUS DOG
Don't know where I'm from,

FRANCESCA FROG
Can't say where I'm goin'.

CIRILLO CAT
Who'd guess my primordial roots
Were slimy and green?

RENALDO, ROSSINI and RACHEL
Oh, genes, dominant genes,

SOLANGE and SIEGFRIED *join in*
Wonderful genes,

DEMETRIUS, FRANCESCA, and CIRILLO *join the others*
Glorious genes!

GENEALOGY OVERTURE

Other animals join in the genealogy quest.

CLARESSA CAT
I think my father was a Siamese.

DEMETRIUS DOG
I think my mother was a Malinois.

CECIL CRAWFISH
I think my gene pool is completely filled with mud.

RAISA RABBIT
The only roots I need are carrots, yams, and spuds.

ESME EAGLE
I think my ancestors migrated west.

PERCIVAL 'POSSUM
I think my granny dangled by her tail.

SIEGFRIED SQUIRREL
I think I shouldn't look too far up in my tree.

RACHEL RAT
Sometimes it's not so great to know your family.

RACHEL and ROSSINI RAT, *as they fire a ship's cannon, taking turns*
Boom! Dadada   *(Cannon fired once, by Rachel)*
Dada dada dadada!

Boom! Dadada   *(Cannon fired a second time, but shot goes wide*
Dada dada dadada!   *as the two rats fight for control)*

SOLANGE SQUIRREL, *ducking as the second cannonball knocks leaves off the limb a
                    above her*
Hey! *grumpily*
Hey-y-y! *in pleased tone, as she finds a plump acorn shaken loose by the cannonball*

I ENJOY BEING A SQUIRREL

The female squirrel grabs the fallen acorn before her mate reaches it, and she proudly holds it high. As each squirrel sings, it darts in front to upstage the other squirrel.

SOLANGE SQUIRREL
When I find a plump new acorn,

SIEGFRIED SQUIRREL, *rubbing his paws down his tail, preening*
And my tail's fluffy and unfurled,

SOLANGE, *leaning against a slanted tree limb*
With a strong, leafy limb to lounge on,

SOLANGE and SIEGFRIED, *nudging each other to gain the front position*
I enjoy being a squirrel.

SOLANGE
When the hickory nuts are ripening,
And the fig tree is filled with fruit,

SIEGFRIED
We can forage for lunch like lightning,
And get home safe with our loot.

SOLANGE, *dancing around with the acorn as Siegfried tries to snatch it*
Lalala lalalala lala,
Lalala lalala lala,
Lalala lalalala lala,
Oh, it's swell being a squirrel,

SIEGFRIED, *briefly gaining possession of the acorn*
Boy squirrel and

SOLANGE, *grabbing the acorn*
Girl

SOLANGE and SIEGFRIED, *both holding onto the acorn*
Squirrel, too!

I'M GETTING FEATHERS

Feathers fall upon the heads of the squirrels, from the tree above them.

DEMOSTHENES DOVE, *après the Wicked Witch of the West in* <u>The Wizard of Oz</u>
I'm molting ... molting!

DONATELLA DOVE
He once was an elegant male.

SOLANGE and SIEGFRIED SQUIRREL
Now he's not so vain.

DONATELLA
Beside him the other doves paled.

SOLANGE and SIEGFRIED, ROSSINI and RACHEL RAT
Now he's awfully plain.

DONATELLA
He started to molt.
It gave me a jolt.
Now, his head is as bare as a nail's.
Coo-oo-oo!

DEMOSTHENES
You have to admit I'm growing feathers,
I'm sprouting feathers all the time.

DONATELLA
He couldn't grow 'em at first.

DEMOSTHENES
Yeah, I'm relieved I'm growing feathers.
I'm getting feathers,
Getting all new feathers all the time.

DONATELLA, SOLANGE, SIEGFRIED, ROSSINI, and RACHEL
He's getting feathers all the time.
Feathers, feathers, feathers!

(I'M GETTING FEATHERS)

DEMOSTHENES, *preening*
I'm getting feathers and I'm fine.

DONATELLA, SOLANGE, SIEGFRIED, ROSSINI, and RACHEL
Feathers, feathers, feathers!

DEMOSTHENES, DONATELLA, SOLANGE, SIEGFRIED, ROSSINI, and RACHEL
Getting all new feathers all the time.

FRESH POULTRY

The cats and dogs have crept close to the doves, rats, and squirrels.

CIRILLO CAT
I love the sensation
Of feathers and bone
Upon my tongue as
I carry my quarry home.

DONATELLA DOVE, *holding up a shielding wing*
Oh, no, you don't!
We're not canapes.
Go somewhere else for prey.

Shoo!

DEMOSTHENES DOVE, *waving his wings*
Away! Just go away!
You'll have to find something else
To kill and eat today.

CLARESSA CAT, *creeping closer to the doves*
But I like fresh poultry.

CIRILLO, *growling at the doves*
Gr-r-r.

DEMETRIUS DOG
Oh, yes, I do, also!

CLARESSA and CIRILLO, *jealously standing between the dog and their potential prey*
Gr-r-r.   *(the doves), growling at the dog*

DEMOSTHENES, *in front of his mate, throwing out his chest in a show of bravado*
Well, your love's unrequited,

DEMOSTHENES and DONATELLA, *distancing themselves from the predators*
And we're flying away.

JUST ENOUGH

The doves, safe for the moment, eye the predators. The rabbits, squirrels, and rats draw near.

DONATELLA DOVE
I've surely had my fill of being seen as someone's dinner.

DEMOSTHENES DOVE
They call us plump and juicy. Would it help if we were thinner?

RAISA RABBIT
I don't think carnivores and omnivores can be dissuaded.

SOLANGE SQUIRREL
They have small, one-track minds.

RACHEL RAT, *moving next to Solange to add,*
They're only safe when they're evaded.

CLARESSA CAT
Saw all the birdies through the window as I ate my luncheon.
Popped through the screen to have a closer look and do some munchin'.

CIRILLO CAT
Warm poultry tartare is a savory treat, there's no denying.
But I've espied one human's recipe I'm up for trying.

Poultry pie!
A hundred thrushes and wrens would be just enough.
It won't need a crust.

CLARESSA
Poultry pie!

CIRILLO
A dozen cardinals thrown in for that special touch …

CLARESSA
And two juicy doves.

(JUST ENOUGH)

CIRILLO
No crust,

CLARESSA
No need for crust,

CIRILLO
Birds are enough, don't want a crust!

RACHEL RAT
I had the munchies, thought I'd scrounge a little in the dumpster.
Found some saltines and peanut butter – sure to make me plumper.
I heard a rustle in the bushes. 'Neath the porch I darted.
Banged my poor noggin on the railing. Gee, that really smarted.

PERCIVAL 'POSSUM, *from his nest beneath the scrub palm*
Though I'm called omnivore, and savor eggs upon occasion,
I'm just as happy with a fruit plate or a box of raisins.
Can't say I find the prospect of a game hunt 'specially thrilling.
A slice or two of bread and pizza crusts are good and filling.

Why eat doves?

SOLANGE
A mound of nutmeats and seeds can be meal enough.

RACHEL, ROSSINI RAT, DONATELLA, and DEMOSTHENES
Plenty enough, plenty enough, plenty enough!

PERCIVAL
And what's wrong with crust?

CIRILLO
I want doves!
A dozen baked in a pie wouldn't be too much.

CIRILLO AND CLARESSA
Never a crust, just wriggly doves.

(JUST ENOUGH)

CIRILLO
I love my doves.
I won't give 'em up.

SIEGFRIED SQUIRREL, RENALDO RABBIT, RACHEL, ROSSINI, RAISA, and SOLANGE
Don't eat doves!

PERCIVAL
Just fill up on cottage cheese. It'll be enough.

ALL ANIMALS EXCEPT THE CATS, DOGS, and EAGLES
Plenty enough, plenty enough, plenty enough!

RENALDO
The killing must stop!

CIRILLO
Doves, doves, doves!

CLARESSA
In pies with thrushes and wrens would be just enough.

The prey animals move further from the cats.

MY FLAVORED THINGS

The cats and dogs mill around, licking their lips and looking sorry to have missed out on a snack. Other animals gingerly move to join them, to discuss pleasant things.

PERCIVAL 'POSSUM, *calling out from his nest*
Sunflower seeds that are already shelled out,

DEMOSTHENES DOVE, *calling from the bushes*
Big hunks of bread whose location is yelled out,

SEAGULL and CROW CALLS, *from overhead*
Here! Here, here!

ROSSINI RAT
Roomy, dark nests decorated with bling …

DONATELLA DOVE
I prefer mine made with pine straw and string.

DEMETRIUS DOG
Great meaty bones I can bury to ferment,

CLARESSA CAT
Spacious backyards where I torment the vermin,

RACHEL RAT
Hey!

SOLANGE SQUIRREL, *trying to loop a rope with cowbell over female cat's head*
Kitties with collars with small bells that ring …

THOR TURTLE, *calling from the surf*
I think that fish is my favorite thing.

FAISAL FISH, *calling from the water hole*
Hey!

RENALDO and RAISA RABBIT
When the hawk glides,

(MY FLAVORED THINGS)

FRANCESCA and FERDINAND FROG
When the sssnake ssslides,

RACHEL RAT
When I'm awfully scared,

SIEGFRIED SQUIRREL
I grab a quick meal and race back to my nest,

ALL ANIMALS (except the eagles)
And then things don't seem so weird.

MAD ABOUT BERRIES

There is further discussion about favorite things.

DONATELLA DOVE
I'm just mad about berries,

DANTE DEER
And I go ga-ga for greens.

TESSA TURTLE
I love small fish that wriggle.

FAISAL FISH
Hey!

RAISA RABBIT
I'm wild for young lima beans.

ESME EAGLE
I like chubby young mammals.

RAISA
Hey!

CASSANDRA CRAWFISH
I favor plankton and krill.

FERDINAND FROG
I love flies and small insects.

SOLANGE SQUIRREL
I find fresh pecans a thrill.

PERCIVAL 'POSSUM, *with sad demeanor*
I'm delighted with dairy.
My dear departed was, too. Sniff, sniff …honk! *(blows his nose, and remains blue)*

CLARESSA CAT
Oh, I'm enamored of seafood.

(MAD ABOUT BERRIES)

DEMETRIUS DOG
And I'll eat anything,
Just love everything!
Fling it all in a stew!

ALL ANIMALS, *in disgust*
Euwh!

CIRILLO CAT, *(spoken, rather than sung)*
Hey, I'm hungry!

ALL ANIMALS (except the opossum), *looking left and right, at each other*
How about you?

GIRL MARSUPIAL

The animals, aware of Percival 'Possum's depressed aspect, gather around to pat him on the back and otherwise sympathize. He responds by telling his sad tale of loss. During it, the others occasionally, one at a time, dart off towards the Rover Street sign and disappear. Each returns with a small scavenged bit of food.

PERCIVAL 'POSSUM
I met a girl marsupial on the eve of the harvest moon
In front of the garbage bin.
She was painfully thin.
'Twas love at first sight.

I gave her a juicy drumstick I'd found, and the treasures of the next few nights,
And soon she looked healthier,
And – like me, I fear –
As plump as a tick.

I loved her, and she could tolerate me.
We roamed through the nights as one.
One rainy morning she vanished.
I've looked high and low to find her.

She has silver fur and a prehensile tail,
And on her long, white face, dark streaks frame
Glorious, gleaming Asian eyes.

Hunters' snares, I fear, have taken her. But in case she's not been eaten,
I'll wait in our nest 'neath the scrub palm, so please …
If you see my girl marsupial,
Tell her I have fresh bananas, and
String cheese.

By the end of his account, the prey animals are sniffling and wiping their eyes, and even the predators seem contemplative.

HAVE YOURSELF A BERRY-FLAVORED YOGHURT

As the animals continue to console the mourning opossum, they present assorted food items that they have scavenged from a party at the humans' home on a nearby street. They offer the treats to Percival.

RACHEL RAT
Have yourself a berry-flavored yoghurt.
Found it in the trash.
Guess those folks on Rover Street had quite a bash.

DIANA DOG
Have yourself a berry-flavored yoghurt.
Eat away the blues.
We have lots of goodies, so
You're free to choose.

RENALDO RABBIT
Sometimes girls wander far from home,
Searching for a crumb or two.
Soon she'll miss her beloved one,
And come wandering home to you.

CLARESSA CAT
Try a taste of cottage cheese and melon.
It'll cheer you up.
I find things look brighter every time I sup.

ALL RATS, DOGS, RABBITS, AND CATS
So, have yourself a berry-flavored yoghurt cup.

Percival accepts the yoghurt cup.

BRIE NEARLY WAS MINE

The opossum munches moodily, as the other animals survey their bounty. They also nibble, and recount the many foods (at the humans' party) that they couldn't quite reach to steal.

DIANA DOG
One honey-baked ham,

CECIL CRAWFISH
One plate full of caviar.

RACHEL RAT
While the partiers hugged the bar,
Brie nearly was mine.

SIEGFRIED SQUIRREL
One bowl of pecans,

CIRILLO CAT
One platter of lobster meat.

ELGAR EAGLE, *swooping onto the scene and causing the other animals to draw back*
One furball with bony feet –
This soon will be mine.

THE HOLES ARE ALIVE

A voice rings out from one of the prey animals' holes.

ROSSINI RAT
The holes are alive
With the –

RAISA RABBIT, *calling out from her own hole*
Shut it!

HUNKY-DORY

The prey animals creep cautiously out of their shelters, looking around for the eagle. Elgar Eagle is at a distance behind them, for the moment. Renaldo Rabbit and Rachel Rat are reluctant to exit their nests. They are encouraged by their mates to be brave.

RAISA RABBIT
Hey! Baby, it's safe to roam.

RENALDO RABBIT
Maybe it's safer home.

ROSSINI RAT, *yelling from the dumpster*
Gravy and rice and rolls!

RACHEL RAT
Maybe I'll take a stroll,
And hit the bin.

RENALDO
Me, I'm staying in.

RACHEL
Hey! 'Taters and bits of fish!

CASSANDRA CRAWFISH
Hey! This flounder tail's delish!

DONATELLA DOVE, *venturing out from beneath a palmetto limb*
Maybe a seed or two ...

DEMOSTHENES DOVE, *staying under the palmetto*
I'm eating grubs, but you
Go right ahead.
Just don't end up dead.

RAISA
We'll be hunky-dory.

ROSSINI
It's just the age-old fight-or-flight story.

(HUNKY DORY)

RAISA
We'll take it day by day,
And stay
Near home, so when they come
We can run underground.

RAISA and RENALDO, RACHEL and ROSSINI, CECIL and CASSANDRA,
DEMOSTHENES and DONATELLA
We'll be hunky-dory.
It's just the story of our survival.
Can't forage far or fight
Our rivals,
Lest predators creep near,
Ready to take us down.

RENALDO, *softly, fading off*
We'll be hunky-dory. ...

MARCH OF THE HAWKS AND EAGLES

"The Fern Dance"
Prey animals engage in a stately procession throughout their habitat, occasionally hiding behind enormous fans made of fern fronds and palmetto limbs. Some fans are various shades of green. Others are pale yellow, reddish-orange, and bronze.

SOLANGE and SIEGFRIED SQUIRREL
When the hawks and eagles arrive,
We must run away and hide.　　　　*At the word "run", the fans are opened.*
With raptors overhead,　　　　　　*The animals stop the procession.*
We're better off in bed.　　　　　　*They gently wave the fans back and forth.*

There are many hours in the day
When we can search for food and play. *The fans are flipped behind the animals and*
So we'll just rest our heads　　　　*then returned to front, held open as shields.*
Till the eagle's flown away.

FIONA and FAISAL FISH, *from the water hole*
Simply disappear
When your senses tell you danger's near.
'Tis a healthy modicum of fear　　　*The animals, one after another, lower fans.*
That will see you through.

ROSSINI and RACHEL RAT, *from the bow wreckage*
Better to stay　　　　　　　　　　*The rats restart the procession eastward.*
A little hungry for a day　　　　　*The others follow, fans held low at right side.*
Than to end up as a fresh entrée
For an eagle's brood.　　　　　　　*The cats, dogs, eagles fall in behind others.*

DEMOSTHENES and DONATELLA DOVE
When the hawks and eagles arrive,
We must run away and hide,　　　　*The fans rise again, waved gently.*
In burrows, downs, and trees,
In cotes and nests and eaves.

ELGAR EAGLE, *from the procession's end, spreading his golden wings*
I can glide for hours on end,　　　*He stalks forward, golden wings contrasted*
Till they venture out, and then,　*against the colored fans behind him.*
As silent as the breeze,
I dive, and dine again.　　　　　　*He swoops around and exits. Fans tremble.*

EASY TO FIND SEEDS

Elgar eagle reappears above, joining his mate in their nest. The prey animals slowly resume their activities, making their way, one by one, to the ramshackle screened porch. The open fans are propped against the pilings that support the porch, to form a cluster of colorful ferns and palmetto limbs.

ROSSINI RAT
Why must eagles be so vicious?
Why must eagles be so mean?
Easy to eat grains,
Easy to find seeds.

RACHEL RAT
Why must eagles be so wicked?
Why must they pursue our kin?
Easy to find roadkill,
Easy to raid garbage bins.

DEMOSTHENES DOVE
What's wrong with worms, or
Nice green vegetation?
Why can't they eat weevils,
Or other bad insects?

DEMOSTHENES and DONATELLA DOVE
Should they only care about their feeding times?
How about our beating hearts?
We need our hearts.

RAISA RABBIT
Why don't eagles become vegans?
They know we are living things.
Shouldn't they eat nuts?
Easy to find seeds.
Shouldn't we survive?
Shouldn't we grow old?

GOLDEN EAGLE/SIMPLY A NEST

From their aerie, the male eagle demonstrates his natural weaponry. The female eagle, amused at her mate's self-admiration, takes a more practical approach.

GOLDEN EAGLE

ELGAR EAGLE
Golden wings ablaze with sunlight,
Golden feet with pearly claws,
Vicious beak as sharp as razors –
Its mighty snap gives all the groundlings pause. *He snaps his beak once. The other animals cringe.*

Every beat from my great wingspan *He flaps his wings a few times.*
Pounds like thunder on the wind.
I grab dinner in my talons
And to my aerie throne ascend.

SIMPLY A NEST

ESME EAGLE
It's simply a nest ...

ELGAR
Bigger than all the rest.

ESME
Big enough to hold a brood
Of little baldy-headed eaglets. *Three small eaglets (puppets) pop up and as quickly drop from sight.*

It's merely a nest,
Made of strong sticks and down,
High above the open plain,
No other nests for miles around.

Simply a nest!

NEST IN DORMERS

The doves step out of the shrubbery as the last note of the female eagle's song sounds overhead.

DEMOSTHENES and DONATELLA DOVE
Nest in dormers,
Nest in dormers.

DONATELLA
We love to raise our little ones
In windows high above the ground,

DEMOSTHENES
In hollow burls and leafy crooks,
In attics and in rafter nooks ...
Far from those hungry looks.

DONATELLA
When raptors circle overhead,
Our little ones won't end up dead –

Fast food for hawks and owls.
We just can't bear the yowls,
Thus lay our eggs in cowls
Of straw and moss and string.

DEMOSTHENES
We only hope for peace
And little piles of seeds.
They're our modest needs.

When hungry felines stalk our drove,
We run to safety in a grove

Of sheltering magnolias.

DONATELLA
Then, with softly whistling wings,
We fly back to our nests
Of straw and moss and string,

(NEST IN DORMERS)

DEMOSTHENES and DONATELLA
And we sing,
To our o-o-off-spri-i-ing. *The two doves snuggle together and walk away.*

BIRD POO BECOMES YOU

The female dog rolls upon the ground where the doves were just standing. Her mate joins her and considers her face with admiration.

DEMETRIUS DOG
Bird poo becomes you,
It mats up your hair,
And forms little crusts
Behind your cute ears.

DIANA DOG
Bird poo becomes me,
I reek with delight.

DEMETRIUS
Why, I could sit here
And smell you all night.

You're all decked out to go roamin',
But Roamer, promise me, dear,
When you're out in the gloamin',
Drag all those road-kills back here.

If I should roll, too,
I hope that you know,
I prefer road-kill over bird poo,
Although …

Bird poo becomes you so.

DIANA
Road-kill becomes you so.

DIANA and DEMETRIUS
Rolling's such fun, you know.

BLOWFLIES OVER THE ROAD-KILL ON ROVER

Demetrius disappears. Moments later he reappears, with his fur slicked back. Other animals recoil as he passes. The crawfish scurry to the edge of the marsh.

CECIL CRAWFISH
There'll be blowflies over
The road-kill on Rover,
When Rover rolls.
Yeah, you wait and see.

There'll be insect action,
And slimy attraction
When tissues reach
Fluidity.

CASSANDRA CRAWFISH
The maggots will writhe and squirm,
The flies will buzz overhead,
There won't be much left that's firm
Of the poor thing that wound up dead.

CECIL
There'll be quite an odor from
That road-kill on Rover.
Tomorrow, just 'cause
That's Day Three.

FLIES BE GONE

The cats and fish join the crawfish in remarking on the canine stench. The opossum makes a comment.

PERCIVAL 'POSSUM, *sotto voce from his nest, après* <u>The Sixth Sense</u> *(film)*
I smell dead people.

CIRILLO CAT
Think the pup could use a dip.

CLARESSA CAT
Needs to give those flies the slip.
Soap and water will do him right.

CIRILLO
He won't go without a fight.

FIONA FISH, *from the water hole*
Don't bring that mutt here to scrub!
This is our home – not a tub.
Soap is not conducive to the quality
Of our health and harmony.

FAISAL FISH
Nae, a smelly dog and sudsies shouldn't be
In our little corner of the deep blue sea.

IT'S A SWELL TIDE FOR SWIMMING

The cats and dogs wander off. The fish celebrate their narrow escape from soap and stench. They move from the water hole via the marsh to the sea at the ark's bow.

FIONA FISH
It's a swell tide for swimming.
I think I'll take a leap.
The moon is near full and it has quite a pull.
I'm happy tonight's tide's not neap.

FAISAL FISH
It's a swell tide for swimming.
I think I'll take the plunge.
The water's so high that it laps at the sky,
And washes the marshes of grunge.

FIONA
Maybe it isn't the sea,

FAISAL
Maybe it's not the salt air,

FIONA
Maybe it isn't the fresh green spartina –
A fish could dine nicely there.

FAISAL
Maybe it's not all the stars
Sprinkling the ocean with gems.
Maybe – just maybe – the reason I'm swimming
Is simply a fishy whim.

FIONA
It's a swell night for swimming.
The moon is shimmery blue.
The water's so high I can swim to the sky,
And bring home a planet or two.

FIONA and FAISAL
Life's great in the deep blue.

SILVER MINNOWS

As the fish frolic in the surf, the sea turtles edge nearer to them. The fish scoot into the marsh for safety.

THOR TURTLE
Silver minnows,
Those silver minnows,
They don't do nothin'
But swim in circles.
I slurp those minnows,
And keep on paddlin' along.

TESSA TURTLE
They'd be better
If they were bigger.

THOR
But they beat nothin',
Or so I figger.
I eat those minnows,
And just keep swimmin' along.

SOMEWHERE IN MY TAD- OR EGGHOOD

Missing out on the fleeing fish, the turtles turn their attention to frogs sitting at marsh's edge. The frogs leap onto land, where they assume they will be safe. A pair of humans shed doubt on that assumption. The male human, wearing a chef's hat, holds an enormous meat cleaver. The female human holds a large fry pan. Both humans are dull-looking and their jaws are slick with saliva.

FRANCESCA FROG
I might have been a naughty tadpole,

FERDINAND FROG
I may have been a devilish egg,

FRANCESCA and FERDINAND
But somewhere in our naughty, devilish youth,
We grew ourselves some mighty fine legs.   *They roll up their pants and admire each other's legs.*

And there you stand,   *They look over their shoulders and*
Butter and   *whirl around to face Henley and*
Pan in hand,   *Hetta, the humans.*
Planning to sear our gams.

But somewhere in our egg- or tadhoods,
We learned when to go on the lam.   *They dash aside to avoid a swipe of the cleaver.*

Nothing good can come from
Humans wielding knives.

And somewhere in our naughty tadhoods,
We learned how to leap for our lives.   *The frogs leap out of sight, with salivating humans shuffling after.*

WHAT A WICKED COOK IS MAN

All, except the dozing opossum, lament the human as omnivore.

FIONA FISH
What a wicked cook is man,
How dangerous with condiments.

FAISAL FISH
He fries our friends and family,

TESSA TURTLE
He marinates and macerates our ma-a-ates.

RENALDO and RAISA RABBIT
He raids our nests and tunnels dark.
He nabs our loved ones whi-i-ile they sleep.

ELGAR EAGLE
The scion of the omnivores,

CLARESSA CAT
The antichrist of animals.

CECIL CRAWFISH
I lie awake,
And fret about the smell of boiling flesh.

CASSANDRA CRAWFISH
I dream of chef's hats chasing me-e-e
Through gleaming cutlery.

DANTE DEER
I fear I'll wake to find myself
In fresh chili.

RACHEL RAT
I toss and turn in turmeric,
And flee from coriander
Ground with peppers hot.

(WHAT A WICKED COOK IS MAN)

DIANA DOG
It's not a farfetched fear as long as
Fowl and small mammals are
Fair game for
The humans.

DEMOSTHENES DOVE
What a beastly cook is man,
How vile he is with condiments.

OKRA GUMBO!

It becomes clear that the humans are Cajuns.

SOLANGE and SIEGFRIED SQUIRREL
O-o-o-o-okra gumbo
Is a dish we desperately avoid.
It's a Cajun treat
That can't be beat
Unless you're the meat to be employed.
Oy!

ROSSINI and RACHEL RAT
O-o-o-o-okra gumbo!
They'll throw ANYTHING into the pot. *(spoken, rather than sung)*
Rabbit, squirrel, and dove,

PERCIVAL 'POSSUM
(Sniff) My lady love, *(spoken, rather than sung)*

FAISAL FISH
Crawfish, too – they'll shove in the whole lot.

DEMOSTHENES and DONATELLA DOVE, CECIL and CASSANDRA CRAWFISH, and RENALDO and RAISA RABBIT
We belong in the air, sea, and land.
Not a PAN! *(spoken, rather than sung)*

CECIL CRAWFISH, *in a pouting tone*
Don't want sauce 'neath our feet ... only sand.

ALL ANIMALS
So when we say,

DESDEMONA DEER
"It's a Cajun!"
Run away! *(yelled, rather than sung) The animals shriek and run towards hiding places, then drift forward again while singing*

ALL ANIMALS
You'll soon be smellin'

(OKRA GUMBO!)

Cauldrons of thick okra gumbo.
Okra gumbo, no way!

O-K-R-A GUM-B-O ...
Okra gummmbo! NO!

I 'SPECT THAT'S WHY THEY CALL IT A STEW

The stirred-up crowd becomes contemplative about its potential fate. The deer put voice to the fears of the many, as they stroll slowly through the habitat.

DESDEMONA DEER
All the deer in the woods know that it's good
To hide their young fawns.
They graze early evening and only come out again
In the first hour of dawn.

They don't consume more than they need
To get by … Oh, my!
'Cause greed only leads to suffering and pain
When those hunters creep back again.

DESDEMONA and DANTE DEER
An' I 'spect that's why they call it a stew.
Hold still for long, and they'll cleave you in two.
Cackling like crazies, stirring and seasoning,
Boiling our babies beyond all reasoning.

DESDEMONA
An' I 'spect that's why they call it a stew.

DANTE
Little mammals and fowl watch for the owl
And the hawk.
And they avoid those humanoids
Who pretend just to stand 'round and gawk.

They don't hesitate for one extra minute
Over the veggies and seeds.
'Cause greed only leads to suffering and pain
When those trappers set their vile snares again.

DESDEMONA and DANTE
An' I 'spect that's why they call it a stew.
Hold still for long, and they'll cleave you in two.
Cackling like crazies, stirring and seasoning,
Boiling our babies beyond all reasoning.

(I 'SPECT THAT'S WHY THEY CALL IT A STEW)

DESDEMONA
An' I 'spect that's why they call it a stew.

DANTE
Cackling like crazies, stirring and seasoning.

DESDEMONA
An' I 'spect that's why they call it a stew.

DANTE
Cackling like crazies, stirring and seasoning.

DESDEMONA
An' I 'spect that's why they call it a stew.

LUNCHEON FARE

The contemplation continues, as the prey acknowledge the predators have their own struggles in life.

RAISA RABBIT
Sometimes life is
Hard to bear,
When we're thought of solely
As luncheon fare.

Still, our hearts grow warm
With our kindred near,
And we know carnivores
Have their own cares.

A BEATING HEART

The predators respond to the sympathy.

DEMETRIUS DOG
Stalking a meal that's moving,
Halting a beating heart –
It gives a thrill, our bellies fill,
But then we're back at the start.

CLARESSA CAT
Life is an endless safari,
Pursuing elusive game.
We pace, and lay in wait for prey.
Each day is just the same.

It's hard to tame
Our hunger pains –
Night and day, it's the same.
Night and day, just the same.

I FEEL ICKY

The male cat, looking peaked and clutching his abdomen, joins his mate.

CIRILLO CAT
I feel icky,
Awful sicky,
One sick kitty,
I'm gritty and grey.
'Tis a pity,
Tossing tuna in this wasteful way.

I feel bilious.

ALL ANIMALS
He's so bilious.

CIRILLO
Supercilious this furball may be,   *(a double entendre) He gestures at*
But it's seriously   *the female cat.*
Bringing out the worst in me.

Ack ... ack ... aaack!   *He gags repeatedly.*

CATPAN

As the male cat gags, the female, with a mild look of disgust, haughtily paces away from him and toward the screened porch. She gestures to the litter box at the porch's end. Near it, the human female is lying on a chaise, covered with a blanket pulled up to her chin.

CLARESSA CAT
If my litter is not policed,
I urinate on my human's fleece. *She waves a paw at the human female.*
And should my human contract the flu,
I conjure up a furball or two.

                                    At this, her mate gags more loudly.
                                    The human female jumps up and runs
CLARESSA and CIRILLO CAT   *indoors, hand covering her mouth.*
Me-ow, me-ow.
Me-ow, me-ow.   *Cirillo staggers off, gagging.*

CLARESSA
Meow, meow, meow, meow,
Meow, meow-meow-meow meow.
Meow, meow, meow, me-ack!
Meow, meow-meow-meo-o-ow, ack! Ack!   *Claressa, too, gags.*

NEITHER A TOM CAT NOR A MOM CAT BE

As both cats crouch near the porch, gagging, the rest of the animals give them advice.

ALL ANIMALS, EXCEPT THE CATS.
Neither a tom cat nor a mom cat be.
Do not forget … go see your vet.

Eat right, and never kill a bird or squirrel.
Don't stray out in the world.

Keep fleas and mites away,
And worms at bay.

Protect your hearts each day.

A PARASITE'S LIFE FOR FLEAS

Tiny voices emanate from the male cat's back. The cat scratches unseen fleas.

VOICES OF BOTH FLEAS
Yee-haw, yahoos!
A parasite's life for fleas.

MALE FLEA VOICE
We suck lots of blood
From their bodies and legs.
Drink up, wee pesties, yee-haw!

FEMALE FLEA VOICE
We leave nasty sores
And lay thousands of eggs.
Lay up, wee pesty yahoos!

VOICES OF BOTH FLEAS
Yee-haw, yahoos!
A parasite's life for fleas.

MALE FLEA VOICE
We slurp, we guzzle,
We gulp, we –
Hey!   *The male flea voice breaks off, as the cat*
                                       scratches.
What the ...   *The male flea voice resumes, more distant,*
                                       as the male rat begins to scratch.

FLEAS MUST GO!

Spurred by the flea transferred to him by the cat's scratching, the rat complains. Other animals join him in a duel of the sexes.

ROSSINI RAT, *unseen, then appearing as he scratches*
Ow, ow-ee, ow, ow-ee, ow, ow-ee, ow, ow, ow …

Fleas must go!
Fleas-must-go, fleas-must-go, fleas-must-go,
Fleas must go!

ROSSINI RAT, CIRILLO CAT, DEMETRIUS DOG, and SIEGFRIED SQUIRREL (THE MALES)
Itchity,

RACHEL RAT, CLARESSA CAT, DIANA DOG, and SOLANGE SQUIRREL (THE FEMALES)
Scratchity,

THE MALES
Itchity,

THE FEMALES
Scratchity,

THE MALES
Itchity,

THE FEMALES
Scratchity,

THE MALES
Itchity,

THE FEMALES
Scratchity.

THE MALES
Itchity,

(FLEAS MUST GO!)

THE FEMALES
Scratchity,

THE MALES
Itchity,

THE FEMALES
Scratchity,

THE MALES
Itchity,

THE FEMALES
Scratchity,
Scratchity,

THE MALES
Itchity.

(Repeat itchity-scratchity verbal duel above.)

THE MALES
Itch,

THE FEMALES
Scratch,
Scratch,

THE MALES
Itch.

Itch,

THE FEMALES
Scratch,
Scratch,

THE MALES
Itch.

(FLEAS MUST GO!)

MALES and FEMALES
Itch, scratch, scra-a-atch, i-i-itch!

HOW DO YOU LOSE A NUISANCE LIKE A FLEA-AH?

A dog and cat ponder a solution to their flea infestation.

DIANA DOG
How do you lose a nuisance like a flea-ah?
How can you rid yourself of nasty pests?
How do you make those fat ol' ticks say, "See ya"?
A passel of powders, or spray in all their nests?

CIRILLO CAT
How do you end the reign of wicked ear mites?
How do you keep the tapey-worms away?

DIANA
When spring comes and pests all hatch,
Beneath fallen leaves and thatch,
They crawl past your knees and latch
Upon your skin.

How do you lose a nuisance like a flea-ah?

DIANA and CIRILLO
How do you keep those creeps from digging in?

I'LL BE FLEAING YOU

The animals find a solution to the problem of pests – their mates. They pair off across the habitat to groom and comfort each other, as the sun sets and the moon rises, throwing all but the lone opossum into silhouette. The opossum is illuminated by the moon once more, his solitude painful as he washes his own little face, scrubbing it half-heartedly with his paws.

CLARESSA CAT
I'll be fleaing you
When crawly things infest your shoulders,
In all the places that you know
Are bugging you.

FAISAL FISH
If you get that bad rot Ich,
I'll paint you with antibiotic.

DANTE DEER
I'll find each fat,
Disgusting deer tick.

DEMOSTHENES DOVE
When lice infest,

DONATELLA DOVE
I'll do my best.

RAISA RABBIT
I'll be fleaing you
In all the spots you cannot reach.
When sand fleas nip you on the beach,
I'll see you through the rash and itch.

SIEGFRIED SQUIRREL
I'll clean your ears of mites and wax,
And scratch your poor back, too.

DEMETRIUS DOG
When I'm howling at the moon,

(I'LL BE FLEAING YOU)

DIANA DOG
I'll still be fleaing you.

DEMETRIUS
How-ow-owl …

The female dog sustains "you" for seven seconds. During seconds three, four, and five, the male dog howls, drifting off as the female finishes.

WALK LIKE AN OPOSSUM

As the moon rises, its circle of light expands. It casts feeble illumination upon a small, misshapen figure emerging from behind the fans at the porch's edge.
The male rat strikes a gong upon the bow of the ark.
The gong sounds again after four seconds. At this second strike of the gong, the male opossum looks up from his grooming and sees the figure at the porch. He rises, and starts in its direction. The female rat softly shakes a tambourine as the male opossum walks in his odd little gait. It becomes obvious that the unknown figure walks with the same gait, and is moving to meet the male.
Their progress is very slow, and all of the female animals begin to shake tambourines fetched from their nests. All of the males shake maracas or rainsticks or play zydeco washboards. The percussive sounds begin low but increase gradually, thumping out the beat of the song.
As the male opossum reaches the other figure, the moon has grown brighter. The other animals realize who the stranger must be.

RACHEL RAT
Yow-ee-yow ...

Yow-ee-yow ...

ALL ANIMALS, EXCEPT THE OPOSSUMS
Ee-yow-ee-yow
Ee-ee-yow-ee-yow!

RACHEL
Walk like an opossum.
Walk like an opossum.

ALL ANIMALS, EXCEPT THE OPOSSUMS
Yow-ee-yow ...

Yow-ee-yow ...

ALL ANIMALS, INCLUDING OPOSSUMS
Ee-yow-ee-yow
Ee-ee-yow-ee-yow!

The opossum clutches the front paws of his long-lost mate. She turns slightly, revealing four little opossums hanging upon her back. He shows great joy. Instruments stop, except for Rachel's lone tambourine.

The other percussive instruments resume and a flute joins, carrying the melody. All of the animals fall in behind the celebratory Percival 'Possum as he holds the arm of his prodigal mate Penelope. The others attempt the 'Possum Pace, a crablike, mambo-esque, jiggling walk.

As the procession roams throughout the habitat, the opossums only have eyes for each other, and Percival cannot stop admiring Penelope and their little offspring.

EE-YOW!

The male opossum, reunited with his lady love, continues to admire her and his newly-introduced offspring, and dances modestly, in a Native American-style double-step. The other animals dance similarly behind him with exuberance, some twirling around. The percussive instrumentation reaches cacophony, and the procession of animals takes on a Junkanoo quality.

PERCIVAL POSSUM
Ee-Yow! Ee-Yow!
Ee-Yow! Ee-Yow!

My lady love's been gone forever.
Now she's home, with everything my poor heart lacked.

My lady, glowing in the moonlight,
With our darling young'uns hangin' on her back! *,counting the babies, by pointing*
Four! *with his paw (silent one-two-three count coincides with words "on her back!")*

Ee-Yow! Ee-Yow!
Ee-Yow! Ee-Yow!

ALL ANIMALS, *dancing*
Ee-Yow! Ee-Yow!
Ee-Yow! Ee-Yow!

LYRICS

SONG LIST

NO-SEE'UMS
IF I ONLY HAD A MATE
PRIDE OF THE PREDATORS
GENES, GLORIOUS GENES
GENEALOGY OVERTURE
I ENJOY BEING A SQUIRREL
I'M GETTING FEATHERS
FRESH POULTRY
JUST ENOUGH
MY FLAVORED THINGS
MAD ABOUT BERRIES
GIRL MARSUPIAL
HAVE YOURSELF A BERRY-FLAVORED YOGHURT
BRIE NEARLY WAS MINE
THE HOLES ARE ALIVE
HUNKY-DORY
MARCH OF THE HAWKS AND EAGLES
EASY TO FIND SEEDS
GOLDEN EAGLE/SIMPLY A NEST
NEST IN DORMERS
BIRD POO BECOMES YOU
BLOWFLIES OVER THE ROAD-KILL ON ROVER
FLIES BE GONE
IT'S A SWELL TIDE FOR SWIMMING
SILVER MINNOWS
SOMEWHERE IN MY TAD- OR EGGHOOD
WHAT A WICKED COOK IS MAN
OKRA GUMBO!
I 'SPECT THAT'S WHY THEY CALL IT A STEW

SONG LIST (continued)

LUNCHEON FARE
A BEATING HEART
I FEEL ICKY
CATPAN
NEITHER A TOM CAT NOR A MOM CAT BE
A PARASITE'S LIFE FER FLEAS
FLEAS MUST GO
HOW DO YOU LOSE A NUISANCE LIKE A FLEA-AH?
I'LL BE FLEAING YOU
WALK LIKE AN OPOSSUM
EE-YOW!

NO-SEE'UMS

Lyrics by Lindy Wall, sung to the music of "Maria",
from the musical <u>West Side Story</u>, music by Leonard Bernstein
(lyrics of original song by Stephen Sondheim)

No-see'ums ...
I just hit a cloud of no-see'ums,
And suddenly it's plain
They've carried my poor brain away.

No-see'ums ...
There's just no escaping no-see'ums.
They get into my ears,
And places that I dare not say.

No-see'ums ...
Run away when you see them swarming.
Get the spray, or you'll itch until morning.

No-see'ums ...
I find them alarming,
No-see'ums.

IF I ONLY HAD A MATE

Lyrics by Lindy Wall, sung to the music of "If I Only Had A Brain",
from the musical The Wizard of Oz, music by Harold Arlen
(lyrics of original song by E.Y. "Yip" Harburg)

Oh, the water hole is hoppin'.
Everyone is stoppin'
By for a drink.
Got to watch for dogs and owl-ers,
And the other evenin' prowlers,
But I am faster than they think.

Gee, the night is dark and eerie,
And I'm kind of leery
Of wanderin' far from home.
Wouldn't mind bein' nocturnal
If it weren't for this infernal
State of bein' alone.

Dum-de-dum-de-da-de-dada –
Ooh, a ripe banana!
Mm-
Mm-
Mmm!
La-de-da-de-dum-de-doodle,
Here's a pack of ramen noodles!
I shall have them for brunch.

Now the mornin' sun is risin'.
Time to close my eyes, an'
I don't wanna be late.
Oh, my nest is comfy-cozy,
And the whole world would be rosy ...
If I only had a mate.

PRIDE OF THE PREDATORS

*Lyrics by Lindy Wall, sung to the music of "Ride of the Valkeries",
from <u>Die Walkurie,</u> second of four operas comprising the masterwork
<u>Der Ring des Nibelungen</u>, by Richard Wagner*

I am a raptor.
I am descended
From pterodactyls.
I am the best.

I am descended
From mighty tigers.
I am ferocious.

Oh, give it a rest!

Nyah, nyah-nyah-nyah, nyah,
Nyah, nyah-nyah-nyah, nyah …

GENES, GLORIOUS GENES

Lyrics by Lindy Wall, sung to the music of "Food, Glorious Food", from the musical <u>Oliver</u>, music by Lionel Bart (lyrics of original song by Lionel Bart)

Genes, glorious genes!
Your DNA's showin'.
Don't know where I'm from,
Can't say where I'm goin'.

Who'd guess my primordial roots
Were slimy and green?
Oh, genes, dominant genes,
Wonderful genes, glorious genes!

GENEALOGY OVERTURE

Lyrics by Lindy Wall, sung to the music of the
cannon finale of 1812 Overture,
symphony by Pitor Ilyich Tchaikovsky

I think my father was a Siamese.
I think my mother was a Malinois.
I think my gene pool is completely filled with mud.
The only roots I need are carrots, yams, and spuds.

I think my ancestors migrated west.
I think my granny dangled by her tail.
I think I shouldn't look too far up in my tree.
Sometimes it's not so great to know your family.

Boom! Dadada
Dada dada dadada!

Boom! Dadada
Dada dada dadada!

Hey!
Hey-y-y!

I ENJOY BEING A SQUIRREL

Lyrics by Lindy Wall, sung to the music of "I Enjoy Being A Girl",
from the musical Flower Drum Song, music by Irving Berlin
(lyrics to original song by Irving Berlin)

When I find a plump new acorn,
And my tail's fluffy and unfurled,
With a strong, leafy limb to lounge on,
I enjoy being a squirrel.

When the hickory nuts are ripening,
And the fig tree is filled with fruit,
We can forage for lunch like lightning,
And get home safe with our loot.

Lalala lalalala lala,
Lalala lalala lala,
Lalala lalalala lala,
Oh, it's swell being a squirrel,

Boy squirrel and
Girl
Squirrel, too!

I'M GETTING FEATHERS

Lyrics by Lindy Wall, sung to the music of "It's Getting Better",
music by John Lennon and Paul McCartney of The Beatles
(lyrics to original song by John Lennon and Paul McCartney)

I'm molting ... molting!

He once was an elegant male.
Now he's not so vain.
Beside him the other doves paled.
Now he's awfully plain.

He started to molt.
It gave me a jolt.
Now, his head is as bare as a nail's.
Coo-oo-oo!

You have to admit I'm growing feathers,
I'm sprouting feathers all the time.
He couldn't grow 'em at first.
Yeah, I'm relieved I'm growing feathers.
I'm getting feathers,
Getting all new feathers all the time.

He's getting feathers all the time.
Feathers, feathers, feathers!
I'm getting feathers and I'm fine.
Feathers, feathers, feathers!

Getting all new feathers all the time.

FRESH POULTRY

Lyrics by Lindy Wall, sung to the music of "O soave fanciulla",
duet from Act One, Part Two, of the opera La Boheme by Giacomo Puccini
(libretto of original duet and opera by Guiseppe Giacosa and Luigi Illica)

I love the sensation
Of feathers and bone
Upon my tongue as
I carry my quarry home.

Oh, no, you don't!
We're not canapes.
Go somewhere else for prey.

Shoo!
Away! Just go away!
You'll have to find something else
To kill and eat today.

But I like fresh poultry.
Gr-r-r.
Oh, yes, I do, also!
Gr-r-r.

Well, your love's unrequited,
And we're flying away.

JUST ENOUGH

Lyrics by Lindy Wall, sung to the music of "Never Too Much",
music by Luther Vandross
(lyrics of original song by Luther Vandross)

I've surely had my fill of being seen as someone's dinner.
They call us plump and juicy. Would it help if we were thinner?
I don't think carnivores and omnivores can be dissuaded.
They have small, one-track minds. They're only safe when they're evaded.

Saw all the birdies through the window as I ate my luncheon.
Popped through the screen to have a closer look and do some munchin'.
Warm poultry tartare is a savory treat, there's no denying.
But I've espied one human's recipe I'm up for trying.

Poultry pie!
A hundred thrushes and wrens would be just enough.
It won't need a crust.

Poultry pie!
A dozen cardinals thrown in for that special touch ...
And two juicy doves.

No crust, no need for crust, birds are enough, don't want a crust!

I had the munchies, thought I'd scrounge a little in the dumpster.
Found some saltines and peanut butter – sure to make me plumper.
I heard a rustle in the bushes. 'Neath the porch I darted.
Banged my poor noggin on the railing. Gee, that really smarted!

Though I'm called omnivore, and savor eggs upon occasion,
I'm just as happy with a fruit plate or a box of raisins.
Can't say I find the prospect of a game hunt 'specially thrilling.
A slice or two of bread and pizza crusts are good and filling.

Why eat doves?
A mound of nutmeats and seeds can be meal enough.
Plenty enough, plenty enough, plenty enough!
And what's wrong with crust?

(JUST ENOUGH)

I want doves!
A dozen baked in a pie wouldn't be too much.
Never a crust, just wriggly doves. I love my doves.
I won't give 'em up.

Don't eat doves!
Just fill up on cottage cheese. It'll be enough.
Plenty enough, plenty enough, plenty enough!
The killing must stop!

Doves, doves, doves!
In pies with thrushes and wrens would be just enough.

MY FLAVORED THINGS

Lyrics by Lindy Wall, sung to the music of "My Favorite Things",
from the musical <u>The Sound of Music</u>, music by Richard Rodgers
(lyrics of original song by Oscar Hammerstein II)

Sunflower seeds that are already shelled out,
Big hunks of bread whose location is yelled out,
Here! Here, here!
Roomy, dark nests decorated with bling …
I prefer mine made with pine straw and string.

Great meaty bones I can bury to ferment,
Spacious backyards where I torment the vermin,
Hey!
Kitties with collars with small bells that ring …
I think that fish is my favorite thing.
Hey!

When the hawk glides,
When the sssnake ssslides,
When I'm awfully scared,
I grab a quick meal and race back to my nest,
And then things don't seem so weird.

MAD ABOUT BERRIES

*Lyrics by Lindy Wall, sung to the music of "I'm Just Wild About Harry",
music by Eubie Blake
(lyrics of original song by Noble Sissle)*

I'm just mad about berries,
And I go ga-ga for greens.
I love small fish that wriggle.
Hey!
I'm wild for young lima beans.

I like chubby young mammals.
Hey!
I favor plankton and krill.
I love flies and small insects.
I find fresh pecans a thrill.

I'm delighted with dairy.
My dear departed was, too. Sniff, sniff …honk!
Oh, I'm enamored of seafood.
And I'll eat anything,
Just love everything!
Fling it all in a stew!
Euwh!

Hey, I'm hungry!
How about you?

GIRL MARSUPIAL

Lyrics by Lindy Wall, sung to the music of "Frank Mills",
from the musical <u>Hair</u>, music by Galt MacDermot
(lyrics of original song by James Rado and Gerome Ragni)

I met a girl marsupial on the eve of the harvest moon
In front of the garbage bin.
She was painfully thin.
'Twas love at first sight.

I gave her a juicy drumstick I'd found, and the treasures of the next few nights,
And soon she looked healthier,
And – like me, I fear –
As plump as a tick.

I loved her, and she could tolerate me.
We roamed through the nights as one.
One rainy morning she vanished.
I've looked high and low to find her.

She has silver fur and a prehensile tail,
And on her long, white face, dark streaks frame
Glorious, gleaming Asian eyes.

Hunters' snares, I fear, have taken her. But in case she's not been eaten,
I'll wait in our nest 'neath the scrub palm, so please …
If you see my girl marsupial,
Tell her I have fresh bananas, and
String cheese.

HAVE YOURSELF A BERRY-FLAVORED YOGHURT

Lyrics by Lindy Wall, sung to the music of "Have Yourself A Merry Little Christmas",
from the musical <u>Meet Me In St. Louis</u>, music by Hugh Martin and Ralph Blane
(lyrics of original song by Hugh Martin and Ralph Blane)

Have yourself a berry-flavored yoghurt.
Found it in the trash.
Guess those folks on Rover Street had quite a bash.

Have yourself a berry-flavored yoghurt.
Eat away the blues.
We have lots of goodies, so
You're free to choose.

Sometimes girls wander far from home,
Searching for a crumb or two.
Soon she'll miss her beloved one,
And come wandering home to you.

Try a taste of cottage cheese and melon.
It'll cheer you up.
I find things look brighter every time I sup.
So, have yourself a berry-flavored yoghurt cup.

BRIE NEARLY WAS MINE

Lyrics by Lindy Wall, sung to the music of "This Nearly Was Mine",
from the musical South Pacific, music by Richard Rodgers
(lyrics of original song by Oscar Hammerstein II)

One honey-baked ham,
One plate full of caviar.
While the partiers hugged the bar,
Brie nearly was mine.

One bowl of pecans,
One platter of lobster meat.
One furball with bony feet –
This soon will be mine.

THE HOLES ARE ALIVE

Lyrics by Lindy Wall, sung to the music of "The Sound of Music",
from the musical <u>The Sound of Music</u>, music by Richard Rodgers
(lyrics of original song by Oscar Hammerstein II)

The holes are alive
With the –

Shut it!

HUNKY-DORY

Lyrics by Lindy Wall, sung to the music of "Hard Candy Christmas",
from the musical <u>Best Little Whorehouse In Texas</u>, music by Carol Hall
(lyrics of original song by Carol Hall)

Hey! Baby, it's safe to roam.
Maybe it's safer home.
Gravy and rice and rolls!
Maybe I'll take a stroll,
And hit the bin.
Me, I'm staying in.

Hey! 'Taters and bits of fish!
Hey! This flounder tail's delish!
Maybe a seed or two …
I'm eating grubs, but you
Go right ahead.
Just don't end up dead.

We'll be hunky-dory.
It's just the age-old fight-or-flight story.
We'll take it day by day,
And stay
Near home, so when they come
We can run underground.

We'll be hunky-dory.
It's just the story of our survival.
Can't forage far or fight
Our rivals,
Lest predators creep near,
Ready to take us down.

We'll be hunky-dory. …

MARCH OF THE HAWKS AND EAGLES

Lyrics by Lindy Wall, sung to the music of "March of the Siamese Children"
(instrumental), from the musical <u>The King and I</u>, music by Richard Rodgers
(lyrics of musical by Oscar Hammerstein II)

When the hawks and eagles arrive,
We must run away and hide.
With raptors overhead,
We're better off in bed.

There are many hours in the day
When we can search for food and play.
So we'll just rest our heads
Till the eagle's flown away.

Simply disappear
When your senses tell you danger's near.
'Tis a healthy modicum of fear
That will see you through.

Better to stay
A little hungry for a day
Than to end up as a fresh entrée
For an eagle's brood.

When the hawks and eagles arrive,
We must run away and hide,
In burrows, downs, and trees,
In cotes and nests and eaves.

I can glide for hours on end,
Till they venture out, and then,
As silent as the breeze,
I dive, and dine again.

EASY TO FIND SEEDS

*Lyrics by Lindy Wall, sung to the music of "Easy To Be Hard",
from the musical <u>Hair</u>, music by Bob Gaudio
(lyrics of original song by Bob Crewe)*

Why must eagles be so vicious?
Why must eagles be so mean?
Easy to eat grains,
Easy to find seeds.

Why must eagles be so wicked?
Why must they pursue our kin?
Easy to find roadkill,
Easy to raid garbage bins.

What's wrong with worms, or
Nice green vegetation?
Why can't they eat weevils,
Or other bad insects?

Should they only care about their feeding times?
How about our beating hearts?
We need our hearts.

Why don't eagles become vegans?
They know we are living things.
Shouldn't they eat nuts?
Easy to find seeds.
Shouldn't we survive?
Shouldn't we grow old?

GOLDEN EAGLE/SIMPLY A NEST

Lyrics by Lindy Wall, medley sung to the music of "Golden Eye",
music by Bono/The Edge of U2 (lyrics of original song by Bono/The Edge), and
"The Best", music by Holly Knight and Mike Chapman (lyrics of original song by
Holly Knight and Mike Chapman)

GOLDEN EAGLE

Golden wings ablaze with sunlight,
Golden feet with pearly claws,
Vicious beak as sharp as razors –
Its mighty snap gives all the groundlings pause.

Every beat from my great wingspan
Pounds like thunder on the wind.
I grab dinner in my talons
And to my aerie throne ascend.

SIMPLY A NEST

It's simply a nest …
Bigger than all the rest.
Big enough to hold a brood
Of little baldy-headed eaglets.

It's merely a nest,
Made of strong sticks and down,
High above the open plain,
No other nests for miles around.

Simply a nest!

NEST IN DORMERS

*Lyrics by Lindy Wall, sung to the music of "Nessun dorma",
aria from Act Three of the opera <u>Turandot</u>, by Giacoma Puccini,
(libretto of original aria and opera by Giuseppe Adams and Renato Simone)*

Nest in dormers,
Nest in dormers.

We love to raise our little ones
In windows high above the ground,
In hollow burls and leafy crooks,
In attics and in rafter nooks …
Far from those hungry looks.

When raptors circle overhead,
Our little ones won't end up dead –

Fast food for hawks and owls.
We just can't bear the yowls,
Thus lay our eggs in cowls
Of straw and moss and string.

We only hope for peace
And little piles of seeds.
They're our modest needs.

When hungry felines stalk our drove,
We run to safety in a grove

Of sheltering magnolias.
Then, with softly whistling wings,
We fly back to our nests
Of straw and moss and string,

And we sing,
To our o-o-off-spri-i-ing.

BIRD POO BECOMES YOU

Lyrics by Lindy Wall, sung to the music of "Moonlight Becomes You",
music by James Van Heusen and Johnny Burke, for the film <u>The Road To Morocco</u>
(lyrics of original song by James Van Heusen and Johnny Burke)

Bird poo becomes you,
It mats up your hair,
And forms little crusts
Behind your cute ears.

Bird poo becomes me,
I reek with delight.
Why, I could sit here
And smell you all night.

You're all decked out to go roamin',
But Roamer, promise me, dear,
When you're out in the gloamin',
Drag all those road-kills back here.

If I should roll, too,
I hope that you know,
I prefer road-kill over bird poo,
Although …

Bird poo becomes you so.

Road-kill becomes you so.

Rolling's such fun, you know.

BLOWFLIES OVER THE ROAD-KILL ON ROVER

Lyrics by Lindy Wall, sung to the music of
"There'll Be Bluebirds Over The White Cliffs of Dover", music by Walter Kent
(lyrics of original song by Nat Burton)

There'll be blowflies over
The road-kill on Rover,
When Rover rolls.
Yeah, you wait and see.

There'll be insect action,
And slimy attraction
When tissues reach
Fluidity.

The maggots will writhe and squirm,
The flies will buzz overhead,
There won't be much left that's firm
Of the poor thing that wound up dead.

There'll be quite an odor from
That road-kill on Rover.
Tomorrow, just 'cause
That's Day Three.

FLIES BE GONE

Lyrics by Lindy Wall, sung to the music of "Caro Nome" ("Gualtier Maldè!...Caro nome"), aria from Act I, Scene II, of the opera <u>Rigoletto</u> by Giuseppe Verdi (libretto of the original aria and opera by Francesco Maria Piave)

I smell dead people.

Think the pup could use a dip.
Needs to give those flies the slip.
Soap and water will do him right.
He won't go without a fight.

Don't bring that mutt here to scrub!
This is our home – not a tub.
Soap is not conducive to the quality
Of our health and harmony.

Nae, a smelly dog and sudsies shouldn't be
In our little corner of the deep blue sea.

IT'S A SWELL TIDE FOR SWIMMING

*Lyrics by Lindy Wall, sung to the music of "A Grand Night For Singing",
from the musical <u>State Fair</u>, music by Richard Rodgers
(lyrics of original song by Oscar Hammerstein II)*

It's a swell tide for swimming.
I think I'll take a leap.
The moon is near full and it has quite a pull.
I'm happy tonight's tide's not neap.

It's a swell tide for swimming.
I think I'll take the plunge.
The water's so high that it laps at the sky,
And washes the marshes of grunge.

Maybe it isn't the sea,
Maybe it's not the salt air,
Maybe it isn't the fresh green spartina –
A fish could dine nicely there.

Maybe it's not all the stars
Sprinkling the ocean with gems.
Maybe – just maybe – the reason I'm swimming
Is simply a fishy whim.

It's a swell night for swimming.
The moon is shimmery blue.
The water's so high I can swim to the sky,
And bring home a planet or two.
Life's great in the deep blue.

SILVER MINNOWS

*Lyrics by Lindy Wall, sung to the music of "Ol' Man River",
from the musical <u>Showboat</u>, music by Jerome Kern
(lyrics of original song by Oscar Hammerstein II)*

Silver minnows,
Those silver minnows,
They don't do nothin'
But swim in circles.
I slurp those minnows,
And keep on paddlin' along.

They'd be better
If they were bigger.
But they beat nothin',
Or so I figger.
I eat those minnows,
And just keep swimmin' along.

SOMEWHERE IN MY TAD- OR EGGHOOD

Lyrics by Lindy Wall, sung to the music of "Something Good",
from the musical The Sound of Music, music by Richard Rodgers
(lyrics of original song by Oscar Hammerstein II)

I might have been a naughty tadpole,
I may have been a devilish egg,
But somewhere in our naughty, devilish youth,
We grew ourselves some mighty fine legs.

And there you stand,
Butter and
Pan in hand,
Planning to sear our gams.

But somewhere in our egg- or tadhoods,
We learned when to go on the lam.

Nothing good can come from
Humans wielding knives.

And somewhere in our naughty tadhoods,
We learned how to leap for our lives.

WHAT A WICKED COOK IS MAN

Lyrics by Lindy Wall, sung to the music of "What A Piece Of Work Is Man",
from the musical Hair, music by Bob Gaudio
(lyrics of original song taken from Hamlet, II, ii, by William Shakespeare)

What a wicked cook is man,
How dangerous with condiments.
He fries our friends and family,
He marinates and macerates our ma-a-ates.

He raids our nests and tunnels dark.
He nabs our loved ones whi-i-ile they sleep.

The scion of the omnivores,
The antichrist of animals.

I lie awake,
And fret about the smell of boiling flesh.
I dream of chef's hats chasing me-e-e
Through gleaming cutlery.

I fear I'll wake to find myself
In fresh chili.

I toss and turn in turmeric,
And flee from coriander
Ground with peppers hot.

It's not a farfetched fear as long as
Fowl and small mammals are
Fair game for
The humans.

What a beastly cook is man,
How vile he is with condiments.

OKRA GUMBO!

*Lyrics by Lindy Wall, sung to the music of "Oklahoma!",
from the musical <u>Oklahoma!</u>, music by Richard Rodgers
(lyrics of original song by Oscar Hammerstein II)*

O-o-o-o-okra gumbo
Is a dish we desperately avoid.
It's a Cajun treat
That can't be beat
Unless you're the meat to be employed.
Oy!

O-o-o-o-okra gumbo!
They'll throw ANYTHING into the pot.
Rabbit, squirrel, and dove,
(Sniff) My lady love,
Crawfish, too – they'll shove in the whole lot.

We belong in the air, sea, and land.
Not a PAN!
Don't want sauce 'neath our feet ... only sand.

So when we say,
"It's a Cajun!"
Run away!
You'll soon be smellin'
Cauldrons of thick okra gumbo.
Okra gumbo, no way!

O-K-R-A GUM-B-O ...
Okra gummmbo! NO!

I 'SPECT THAT'S WHY THEY CALL IT A STEW

Lyrics by Lindy Wall, sung to the music of "I Guess That's Why They Call It The Blues", music by Elton John, Bernie Taupin, and Davey Johnstone
(lyrics of original song by Elton John, Bernie Taupin, and Davey Johnstone)

All the deer in the woods know that it's good
To hide their young fawns.
They graze early evening and only come out again
In the first hour of dawn.

They don't consume more than they need
To get by ... Oh, my!
'Cause greed only leads to suffering and pain
When those hunters creep back again.

An' I 'spect that's why they call it a stew.
Hold still for long, and they'll cleave you in two.
Cackling like crazies, stirring and seasoning,
Boiling our babies beyond all reasoning.

An' I 'spect that's why they call it a stew.

Little mammals and fowl watch for the owl
And the hawk.
And they avoid those humanoids
Who pretend to stand 'round and gawk.

They don't hesitate for one extra minute
Over the veggies and seeds.
'Cause greed only leads to suffering and pain
When those trappers set their vile snares again.

An' I 'spect that's why they call it a stew.
Hold still for long, and they'll cleave you in two.
Cackling like crazies, stirring and seasoning,
Boiling our babies beyond all reasoning.

An' I 'spect that's why they call it a stew. Cackling like crazies, stirring and seasoning.
An' I 'spect that's why they call it a stew. Cackling like crazies, stirring and seasoning.
An' I 'spect that's why they call it a stew.

LUNCHEON FARE

Lyrics by Lindy Wall, sung to the music of "Un bel di, vedremo",
aria from Act Two, Part One, of the opera <u>Madama Butterfly</u> by Giacomo Puccini
(verses in libretto of the original aria and opera by Guiseppe Giacosa, prose text by
Luigi Illica)

Sometimes life is
Hard to bear,
When we're thought of solely
As luncheon fare.

Still, our hearts grow warm
With our kindred near,
And we know carnivores
Have their own cares.

A BEATING HEART

*Lyrics by Lindy Wall, sung to the music of "O mio barbino caro",
aria from Part One of the opera <u>Gianni Schicci</u> by Giacomo Puccini
(libretto of the original aria and opera by Giuseppe Adami)*

Stalking a meal that's moving,
Halting a beating heart –
It gives a thrill, our bellies fill,
But then we're back at the start.

Life is an endless safari,
Pursuing elusive game.
We pace, and lay in wait for prey.
Each day is just the same.

It's hard to tame
Our hunger pains –
Night and day, it's the same.
Night and day, just the same.

I FEEL ICKY

Lyrics by Lindy Wall, sung to the music of "I Feel Pretty",
from the musical <u>West Side Story</u>, music by Leonard Bernstein
(lyrics of original song by Stephen Sondheim)

I feel icky,
Awful sicky,
One sick kitty,
I'm gritty and grey.
'Tis a pity,
Tossing tuna in this wasteful way.

I feel bilious.
He's so bilious.
Supercilious this furball may be,
But it's seriously
Bringing out the worst in me.

Ack ... ack ... aaack!

CATPAN

Lyrics by Lindy Wall, sung to the music of "Habanera",
aria from Act One of the opera Carmen, by Georges Bizet
(libretto of original aria and opera by Henri Meilhac and Ludovic Halevy)

If my litter is not policed,
I urinate on my human's fleece.
And should my human contract the flu,
I conjure up a furball or two.

Me-ow, me-ow.
Me-ow, me-ow.

Meow, meow, meow, meow,
Meow, meow-meow-meow meow.
Meow, meow, meow, me-ack!
Meow, meow-meow-meo-o-ow, ack! Ack!

NEITHER A TOM CAT NOR A MOM CAT BE

Lyrics by Lindy Wall, sung to the music of "Toreador Song", ("Votre toest ...
Toreador, en garde") from Act II, Scene II, of the opera Carmen by Georges Bizet
(libretto of original opera by Henri Meilhac and Ludovic Halevy) –
"Torreador Song" was also parodied on the television series Gilligan's Island
(using words of Polonius ,"Neither A Borrower Nor a Lender Be ...",
from Hamlet, I,iii, by William Shakespeare)

Neither a tom cat nor a mom cat be.
Do not forget ... go see your vet.

Eat right, and never kill a bird or squirrel.
Don't stray out in the world.

Keep fleas and mites away,
And worms at bay.

Protect your hearts each day.

A PARASITE'S LIFE FOR FLEAS

Lyrics by Lindy Wall, sung to the music of "A Pirate's Life For Me" by George Bruns
(lyrics of original song by Xavier Atencio)

Yee-haw, yahoos!
A parasite's life for fleas.

We suck lots of blood
From their bodies and legs.
Drink up, wee pesties, yee-haw!

We leave nasty sores
And lay thousands of eggs.
Lay up, wee pesty yahoos!

Yee-haw, yahoos!
A parasite's life for fleas.

We slurp, we guzzle,
We gulp, we –
Hey!

What the …

FLEAS MUST GO!

*Lyrics by Lindy Wall, sung to the music of "Largo al factotum",
aria from the opera buffa <u>Il Barbiere di Siviglia</u>, by Gioacchino Rossini
(libretto of original aria and opera by Cesare Sterbini)*

Ow, ow-ee, ow, ow-ee, ow, ow-ee, ow, ow, ow ...

Fleas must go!
Fleas-must-go, fleas-must-go, fleas-must-go,
Fleas must go!

Itchity,
Scratchity,
Itchity,
Scratchity,
Itchity,
Scratchity,
Itchity,
Scratchity.

Itchity,
Scratchity,
Itchity,
Scratchity,
Itchity,
Scratchity,
Scratchity,
Itchity.

(Repeat entire itchity-scratchity verbal duel above.)

Itch,
Scratch,
Scratch,
Itch.

Itch,
Scratch,
Scratch,
Itch.

FLEAS MUST GO!

Itch, scratch, scra-a-atch, i-i-itch!

HOW DO YOU LOSE A NUISANCE LIKE A FLEA-AH?

Lyrics by Lindy Wall, sung to the music of "How Do You Solve A Problem Like Maria", from the musical <u>The Sound of Music</u>, music by Richard Rodgers (lyrics of original song by Oscar Hammerstein II)

How do you lose a nuisance like a flea-ah?
How can you rid yourself of nasty pests?
How do you make those fat ol' ticks say, "See ya"?
A passel of powders, or spray in all their nests?

How do you end the reign of wicked ear mites?
How do you keep the tapey-worms away?

When spring comes and pests all hatch,
Beneath fallen leaves and thatch,
They crawl past your knees and latch
Upon your skin.

How do you lose a nuisance like a flea-ah?
How do you keep those creeps from digging in?

I'LL BE FLEAING YOU

Lyrics by Lindy Wall, sung to the music of "I'll Be Seeing You",
from the musical comedy <u>Right This Way</u>, music by Irving Kahal and Sammy Fain
(lyrics of original song by Irving Kahal and Sammy Fain)

I'll be fleaing you
When crawly things infest your shoulders,
In all the places that you know
Are bugging you.

If you get that bad rot Ich,
I'll paint you with antibiotic.

I'll find each fat,
Disgusting deer tick.

When lice infest,
I'll do my best.

I'll be fleaing you
In all the spots you cannot reach.
When sand fleas nip you on the beach,
I'll see you through the rash and itch.

I'll clean your ears of mites and wax,
And scratch your poor back, too.

When I'm howling at the moon,
I'll still be fleaing you.

How-ow-owl ...

WALK LIKE AN OPOSSUM

Lyrics by Lindy Wall, sung to the music of "Walk Like An Egyptian",
by Liam Sternberg
(lyrics of original song by Liam Sternberg)

Yow-ee-yow …

Yow-ee-yow …

Ee-yow-ee-yow
Ee-ee-yow-ee-yow!

Walk like an opossum.
Walk like an opossum.

Yow-ee-yow …

Yow-ee-yow …

Ee-yow-ee-yow
Ee-ee-yow ee-yow!

EE-YOW!

Lyrics by Lindy Wall, sung to the music of "Hey Ya",
by André Benjamin of Outkast
(lyrics of original song by André Benjamin)

Ee-Yow! Ee-Yow!
Ee-Yow! Ee-Yow!

My lady love's been gone forever.
Now she's home, with everything my poor heart lacked.

My lady, glowing in the moonlight,
With our darling young'uns hangin' on her back!
Four!

Ee-Yow! Ee-Yow!
Ee-Yow! Ee-Yow!
Ee-Yow! Ee-Yow!
Ee-Yow! Ee-Yow!

To order additional copies of this book, as well as the companion guide for set and costume design and stage direction, contact

FUTUROLA, INCORPORATED
P. O. Box 15181
Savannah, Georgia 31416-1881

or, purchase this book and

THE ONE PENNY COMPANION
(Available in spring of 2008)

at any bookstore, or at

www.lulu.com/futurolainc

Lindy Wall is a writer, artist, and animal rescuer.
She lives near Savannah, Georgia, with a
menagerie of wild and domesticated animals.

www.ingramcontent.com/pod-product-compliance
Lightning Source LLC
Chambersburg PA
CBHW021011090426
42738CB00007B/754